MAINE POEMS

BY THE SAME AUTHOR

MAINE POEMS

Richard Eberhart

New York   Oxford
OXFORD UNIVERSITY PRESS
1989

Oxford University Press

Oxford   New York   Toronto
Delhi   Bombay   Calcutta   Madras   Karachi
Petaling Jaya   Singapore   Hong Kong   Tokyo
Nairobi   Dar es Salaam   Cape Town
Melbourne   Auckland

and associated companies in
Berlin   Ibadan

Copyright © 1989 by Richard Eberhart

Published by Oxford University Press, Inc.
200 Madison Avenue, New York, New York 10016

Oxford is a registered trademark of Oxford University Press

Library of Congress Cataloging-in-Publication Data

Eberhart, Richard, 1904–
Maine poems / Richard Eberhart.
p.   cm.
ISBN 0-19-505525-X   ISBN 0-19-505526-8 (pbk.)
1. Maine—Poetry.   I. Title.
PS3509.B456M3   1989
811'.52—dc19   88-735
CIP

2 4 6 8 10 9 7 5 3 1

Printed in the United States of America
on acid-free paper

ACKNOWLEDGMENTS

I am grateful to the editors of the following publications in which some of the poems in this book first appeared: *American Poetry Review, Dartmouth Alumni Magazine, Denver Review, Negative Capability, The New England Review, The New York Quarterly, Partisan Review, The Sewanee Review, The Worcester Review,* and *The Yale Literary Magazine.*

"Sailing to Buck's Harbor" first appeared in *The Yale Literary Magazine,* Vol. 150, No. 1. Reprinted by permission © 1982 by the American Literary Society.

Poems from *The Long Reach* (copyright © 1948, 1953, 1956, 1964, 1967, 1976, 1977, 1978, 1979, 1980, 1981, 1982, 1983, 1984 by Richard Eberhart) are reprinted by permission of New Directions Publishing Corporation.

CONTENTS

MAINE POEMS

OLD TREE BY THE PENOBSCOT

There is an old pine tree facing Penobscot Bay,
On the bank above the tide,
Like a predecessor. Its fate
Will be that of its forebear.
I watched the former tree ten years
While it faced the surge of the sea.

Whelmings of the tide, line storms
Buffeted the root system of the pine
Twenty feet above the tide.
I watched the changes of the seasons,
Each year returning assessed
Somber change, a kind of stalwart declination.

As children grew up the pine tree grew down,
Threw down its length in defiant slowness,
Until one summer it was almost horizontal.
Even then, with jags of dead branches, it clung
To life, until further summers dipped it down
Until it lay a dry myth along the shore.

There is something ominous in the new tree
Erect on the high bank, at the very edge,
The sea's hands pulling out earth from the roots,
Slowly displacing a system of boulders,
As I watch through soft afternoons.
The tides have slowly taken the children away.

Then this new tree, about to begin to fall
Through subtle gradations of the strength of years,
Took on the force of a grisly apparition,
My memory was forced down to defeat,
My riches gone, my corpse on the beach,
Dry bones, dry branches, I too a myth of time.

3

DEATH IN THE MINES

Think of man praying. He raises his hands to God.
Whatever his doubts, he has come to this attitude.
It is a skyward and an outward penetration.
The man praying tries to penetrate mysteries which are heavy,
Which turned his hands downward, to earth, its common work,
In any hope beyond the common disasters of time.

Then I read of the miners of Cape Rosier
Who, descending into the interior of the earth,
Exercised their hands upward to pick the rocks above,
As if they could uncover and pluck some ultimate stone.
Thinking not of Samson pulling down his temple,
They struck (one stroke!) one ore so rich in meaning
Devastation shook, and killed them in a pile of rubble.

They are dead, a common lot. America goes on.
The nation rides on the skin of the planet, multitudinously.
As malfunctioned astronauts might ride around the planet
Dead until they disintegrate to a cinder, a puff
Finally as light and delicate as an April daffodil,
Influential members of mysterious time,
The dead miners in the slow growth of their disintegration

Express the serious, interior reality of poetry.
Ride easy, earth, in your strong contention,
You are stronger than man, and ride us down.
But a wind will spring up, a spirit arise
And ride on the air lightly, supremely clear,
In other centuries, and in other civilizations.

INCHIQUIN LAKE, IRELAND
PENOBSCOT BAY, MAINE

(To Jack and Moira Sweeney)

Galway Jack, Dublin Moira, wild swans,
Flapping the lake water, going a way off,
To settle under the big burren brazoning over there,

You have set your house apart from wildness,
The world to view spectacular,
Scope of history in a picture window.

Within all is warmth, Paddy in the glass,
The fine elicitations of the mind
Spark again your old subtleties.

To have gone back to the old world,
To have escaped from brain-blasting America,
To be an overseer of ancient Ireland!

Here on Penobscot Bay fog comes from the Atlantic,
Pumpkin Island far in mist, half alight
In evening half fog, a heaven pageantry

Of strangest lights and shapes, a drama
Never to come to a conclusion, slow
Drifting occlusion, hundred mile view,

The stealthy nature takes over the land,
Wigwam Indians prepare to fight the white man,
Summer fold see TV Watergate.

COAST OF MAINE

The flags are up again along the coast,
Gulls drop clams from a height onto the rocks,
The seas tend to be calm in July,
A swallow nests under our areaway,
It is high summer, the greatest days of the year,
Heat burgeoning the flowers, stones heating the tides,

This is peace, the indifference of nature, another year
Seeming the same as the year before,
The static ability of the world to endure.
There is Eagle Island twelve miles down the bay,
A mole has just dared to march over our garden,
The far islands seem changeless through decades.

Yet, think of the drama! Here am I,
One year older into inevitability,
The country torn in honor's toss-out,
What does nature care about the nature of man?
Three hundred years ago along this coast
The Europeans came to confront the Indians,

Yet the Ice Age shaped these shores millions
Of years ago, unimaginable upon our senses,
What do I say to the beneficent sun
Descending over the pine trees, the sun of our planet?
What does it care for the nature of man,
Its virile essence unassimilable?

Here come the hummingbirds, messengers
Of fragility, instantaneous as imagination,
How could they be so iridescent-evanescent,
Quick-darters, lovers of color, drinkers of nectar?
Do they remind us of a more spirited world
When everything was lithe, and quick, and visionary?

SEA-HAWK

The six-foot nest of the sea-hawk,
Almost inaccessible,
Surveys from the headland the lonely, the violent waters.

I have driven him off,
Somewhat foolhardily,
And look into the fierce eye of the offspring.

It is an eye of fire,
An eye of icy crystal,
A threat of ancient purity.

Power of an immense reserve,
An agate-well of purpose,
Life before man, and maybe after.

How many centuries of sight
In this piercing, inhuman perfection
Stretch the gaze off the rocky promontory.

To make the mind exult
At the eye of a sea-hawk,
A blaze of grandeur, permanence of the impersonal.

OFF SPECTACLE ISLAND

Seals and porpoises present
A vivid bestiary
Delightful and odd against the mariner's chart.

The sea bells do not locate them,
Nor lights, nor the starred ledges;
We are unprotected from their lyricism.

They play in the blue bay, in day,
Or whoosh under the midnight moonlight;
We go from point to point where we are going.

I would rather see them playing,
I would rather hear them course
Than reach for Folly from Pride's Light.

THE CLAM DIGGERS
AND DIGGERS OF SEA WORMS

Appear far up the cove at low tide,
When the sea floor is a wet mastic,
Four men universal
In bent attitude of work,
Gray, mud-coloured, dun,
Caught in a moment of time
When a secret yield
Is possible to ancient earth—
I see them from a field
Under a cliff,
Almost static, scarcely moving
In their solemn grandeur,
The clam diggers,
The diggers of sea worms,
Placing their rakes down
Hard in the muck,
Loosening, pulling up,
Slowly manoeuvering,
Making rough black lines
In their slow progress
Disturbing the smooth, wet, black
Sea bottom of the cove
As sea animals may be
Making necessary tracks,
Solemn, ancient,

Then they became again
The living gray workers
Honest as surrounding cliffs,
Man making a living
From sea-fat residuums
When the sea has receded,
All gay boats and sails
Far off: earth-rich
Dark, gray men at work,
Impersonal as pines and sky,
I watch the heavy scene,
The slow, mute progress
Of torso, arm, leg and rake
As seeing a dark core
And sombre purpose of life,
Primitive simplicity,
Dignity beyond speech,
My mute salutation,
Time-deepened love
To clam diggers,
The diggers of sea worms.

A SHIP BURNING
AND A COMET ALL IN ONE DAY

When the tide was out
And the sea was quiet,
We hauled the boat to the edge,
On a fair day in August,
As who, all believing,
Would give decent burial
To the life of a used boat,
Not leave a corpse above ground.

And some, setting fires
On the old and broken deck,

9

Poured on the kerosene
With a stately quietude,
Measuring out departure,
And others brought libations
In red glasses to the sea's edge,
And all held one in hand.

Then the Captain arose
And poured spirit over the prow
And the sparks flew upward
And consigned her with fierce
Cry and fervent prayer
To immortal transubstantiation.
And the pure nature of air
Received her grace and charm.

And evening came on the sea
As the whole company
Sat upon the harsh rocks
Watching the tide come in
And take the last debris,
And when it became dark
A great comet appeared in the sky
With a star in its nether tail.

OSPREYS IN CRY

When I heard the call of the osprey,
The wild cries of the ospreys
Breasting the wind high above
The cliff, held static
On updraft over the ocean,
Piercing with ancient, piercing eyes
The far ocean deep

I felt a fleshed exultance
For the fierce, untamed beauty
Of these sea-birds, sea-hawks,
Wild creatures of the air,
Magnificent riders
Of the wind's crests, plummeters
Straight down for prey

Caught under water in talons
Triumphant as life,
The huge birds struggling up
Shaking heavy water off
And powerfully taking the air
With fish in talons head first;

I felt a staggering sense
Of the victor and of the doomed,
Of being one and the other,
Of being both at one time,
I was the seer
And I was revealed.

THE SPIDER

I

The spider expects the cold of winter.
When the shadows fall in long Autumn
He congeals in a nest of paper, prepares
The least and minimal existence,
Obedient to nature. No other course
Is his; no other availed him when
In high summer he spun and furled
The gaudy catches. I am that spider,
Caught in nature, summer and winter.
You are the symbol of the seasons too.

II

Now to expatiate and temporize
This artful brag. I never saw so quieting
A sight as the dawn, dew-clenched foot-
Wide web hung on summer barn-eaves, spangled.
It moves to zephyrs that is tough as steel.
I never saw so finely-legged a creature
Walk so accurate a stretch as he,
Proud, capable, patient, confident.
To the eye he gave close penetration
Into real myth, the myth of you, of me.

III

Yet, by moving eyesight off from this
There is another dimension. Near the barn,
Down meadow to shingle, no place for spiders,
The sea in large blue breathes in brainstorm tides,
Pirates itself away to ancient Spain,
Pirouettes past Purgatory to Paradise.
Do I feed deeper on a spider,
A close-hauled view upon windless meaning,
Or deeper a day or dance or doom bestride
On ocean's long reach, on parables of God?

SEA-RUCK

Washback of the waters, swirl of time,
Flashback of time, swirl of the waters,

Loll and stroke, loll and stroke,

The world remade, the world broken,
Knocked rhythm, make of the slime,

The surge and control, stroke of the time,
Heartbreak healing in the grime, and groaner

Holding its power, holding the hurl,
Loll and hurl, power to gain and destroy,

The tall destruction not to undo

A saffron inevitable sun, far and near,
Some vast control, beyond tear and fear,

Where the blood flows, and nights go,
Man in his makeshift, there is home,

And the dark swells, the everlasting toll,
And being like this sea, the unrolling scroll,

Stroke and loll, loll and stroke, stroke, loll

A MAINE ROUSTABOUT

He was there as the yachts went by

Percy is my name; my accent is good,
I am told, as good as that of an Elizabethan.
I had no schooling beyond the age of sixteen.
My wife left me. I took to drink, live with a dog.
I resent children unless they can hold their own
With grown-ups. I've been around the world on ships,
Down Connecticut way on jobs, once got to Georgia,
Always return to the rocks and the hard times
Of Maine. At clambakes in the summertime
I sit with the summer folk on the conglomerate shore,
Play my old fiddle a sharp tune or two,
Old airs I learned from my brother when we were boys.
It was always tough with me. Sharp as the city folks

I think I am, but am ever wary against them,
Keep my difference, and will not let them tell me off.
I have no respect for their savage villainies,
Yet their power over life always fascinated me.
They own the place. They come and go, I'm left
To chores and dung. But I can catch a mackerel
Almost any afternoon on the incoming tide
With an old hook, when they're running, old line,
In my old boat: they won't take hook from the richlings.
If I scare the children with my grizzled face
It's an old gut forced with whiskey keeps me going.

SEA BURIAL FROM THE CRUISER *REVE*

She is now water and air,
Who was earth and fire.

Reve we throttled down
Between Blake's Point and Western Isle,

Then, oh, then, at the last hour,
The first hour of her new inheritance,

We strewed her ashes over the waters,
We gave her the bright sinking

Of unimaginable aftermaths,
We followed her dispersed spirit

As children with a careless flick of wrist
Cast on the surface of the sea

New-cut flowers. Deeper down,
In the heavy blue of the water,

Slowly the white mass of her reduced bones
Waved, as a flag, from the enclosing depths.

She is now water and air,
Who was earth and fire.

FLUX

The old Penobscot Indian
Sells me a pair of moccasins
That stain my feet yellow.

The gods of this world
Have taken the daughter of my neighbor,
Who died this day of encephalitis.

The absentee landlord has taken over Tree Island
Where one now hesitates to go for picnics,
Off the wide beach to see Fiddle Head.

The fogs are as unpredictable as the winds.
The next generation comes surely on,
Their nonchalance baffles my intelligence.

Some are gone for folly, some by mischance,
Cruelty broods over the inexpressible,
The inexorable is ever believable.

The boy, in his first hour on his motorbike,
Met death in a head-on collision.
His dog stood silent by the young corpse.

Last week, the sea farmer off Stonington
Was tripped in the wake of a cruiser.
He went down in the cold waters of the summer.

Life is stranger than any of us expected,
There is a somber, imponderable fate.
Enigma rules, and the heart has no certainty.

MOMENT OF EQUILIBRIUM AMONG THE ISLANDS

The sea repeats itself in light flourishes,
The southwest breeze-up of the midday
Is a lavish presentiment of possible danger,
Coves beckon as waves attack the prow
And slip past in stubby frenzies of loss.
Then we dare the open ocean; the green swells
We ride over with thorough, lordly motion,
Lovers of wind, sun, and the world-turn horizon,
And seek a new island, with a small spit of sand.
The anchor holds; we climb through contorted woods
Up boulders to an old granite quarry, whose
Dark, green, still, fresh water refutes the ocean.
It is the moment of looking down to still water
From massed granite blocks pleases the soul
With the hardness and fantasy of the world,
Before we must try again the gripping buoyancy
Of the salt sea, whose profound depths
Appear only to the imagination, while eyes
Survey the fresh roads the vessel walks
In triumph of buoyancy, delicacy, and strength,
As a philosopher continuing in the essential.
Then standing to the westward-closing sun
As the wind dies and waves grovel to stillness,
We reach at nightfall the landfall buoy of home.

A WEDDING ON CAPE ROSIER

Today there is another marriage
Of the very young by the side of the sea.
The caterer is so pleasant he seems one of the guests.
The parents are divorced but the yachting young
Take communion along with their vows
In a forest chapel looking out over the ocean.
A small boy strews rose petals one by one,
So delicate and beautiful an operation
As to defy the desires of poetry,
While a dog comes into the service
With rude life to remind us
Of the charm and stability of the animal kingdom,
Which we deny in singing
The praises of life everlasting,
That deepest wisdom of centuries of Christendom
Which speaks for the vanishing of everything present
Although the young couple in their youth's beauty
Could not be more evident, capable, or potential.

Father Emerson puts out the candles.
His father knew Emily Dickinson.

It takes so short a time to get married,
We noticed no change in the tide.

ON RETURNING TO A LAKE IN SPRING

When the new frogs in their exuberant arrivals
By hundreds raised their voices in lusty croaks
As I walked up to my knees in reeds among them,
Wading through the wet strong forces of present nature
As if I felt for the first time a divination
So powerful as to shake my frame beyond words,

And only the small frogs could speak harsh articulation
Of the pure force racking them to ecstasy,
When I strode like a god among the small,
The bright movers, the true, walking in triumph
As a king of the frogs, glad to be among them,
As they touched my legs as I moved along,

I remarked their destiny, their birth and death
As one sure of mine, the minimal existence, here in
The great opening of the world again, sure as I was
Of the summer life, in full sunlight, of frogs and men,
I was equally sure of the fall of the year, winter,
The razoring sleet, and locking ice and snow.

I returned to the picnic on the hill exulting.
In our party a young woman moving in her youth
Seemed to jump at the glory of the springtime;
Nevertheless she did not speak of the spring peepers.
A month later, in a southern bog, she slit her throat.

VAN BLACK, AN OLD FARMER IN HIS DELL

Times of Archaic Splendour that you saw

There are times of archaic splendour that you saw
That when you saw them could not show
The unexaggeratable meaning of their drift
Which appeared in memory with unalterable flow.

You saw truth, you saw reality, the whole scene
Of man on the face of the earth, holding a rake,
And with muscles in his arms as big as baseballs
He pulled the gauze of summer to thick windrows.

It is his care that matters to us in the end,
His bent stance in the glaze of ancient sunlight,

The grueling work as if he had the mastery,
It is his lean tough luckless finicky endeavour

In the swift downfall of the year in August
Makes pathos grand, grand against granite cliffs
That tower above him inhuman, big as time,
Methodically he pulls on the rake's loose teeth,

Up on the cliff at the stealthy end of day
A buck leaps from rocks, held in sky light
An instant, so magical, so graceful, so final
He knows he has seen the glory of the world,

Will never be able to put in words this vision,
A throw of the eye beyond the field of raked nature,
A dazzle of the sense, archaic splendour of action
Lost forever: the buck leaping, the man gone underground.

FROTH

When the sea pours out under the bridge
Over the dam at every outgoing of the tide
There is ravishing serendipity of froth.
I stand on a hundred-year-old millstone.

Froth gathers on the turbulence of the waters
Abundant, fresh, puffed up. For hundreds of feet
Small cliffs, bluffs, towers form and seethe
From the turbulent center outward gliding,

Iimprobable as heaven, like a child's view of heaven.
How could anything so frail seem so permanent,
How could anything so sheer evade destruction,
These are things of imagination floating slowly away,

A white suds against blue water, white over blue,
A too much of nothing strangely become everything,
Froth dominating the presence of the world,
Cliffs, bluffs, towers and castles passing by.

It is good that everything has turned to froth,
Magical froth of truths going out to sea,
While I stand on the millstone solid and gray
I hear the airy shapes whispering infinity.

THE SWALLOWS RETURN

For five years the swallows did not build
In the treehouse near the door facing the sea.
I felt their absence as furtive and wordless.
They were put out of mind because they had to be.

Then they came again, two males attending one female,
Skimming in the late afternoon gracefully, ardent
And free in quick glides and arcs, catching flies on the wing.
Feeding their young in the house safely pent.

It was mid-summer, the time of high July,
Their return as mysterious as their former leaving.
They presented the spectacle of orderly nature,
Their lives to some deep purpose cleaving?

At night there was clamor. When morning came
The ground under the house was littered with feathers.
None knows who was the predator, but death
Is available to birds as to man in all weathers.

THE WEDDING

With a southwest wind blowing late August,
Sally held a young seagull in her two hands.
With a love as supple as youth itself
In an ascending gesture she released the wild bird
In a moment of consummate grace and communion.

For an instant the girl and the bird were one.
Then the wild bird went to the wilderness of air
And the young girl returned to the confines of mankind.
Her gesture was like a release of the spirit
Held within the bounds of the corporeal.

Now we assemble on her wedding day
With no direct analogy in mind.
Bride and bridgroom here throw off the past,
But do they? Does a spirit of freedom hover
Over the future from the hand-held past?

GOING TO MAINE

Going to Maine is a state of mind,
Like everything else.
You may have been on Guemas Island,
In the State of Washington,

Viewing the Cascades wide over water,
Watching an eagle soar,
Impressed with the quantity of water,
And eaten bear steak with the McCrackens,

But when you return to ancient New England
The first question asked on Main Street,
With breathless expectation, is,
Are you going to Maine?

Are you going to Maine, oh,
Are you going to Maine?
And I say, yes, we are going to Maine,
And they say, When?

They want an ultimate answer
To an ultimate question.
Pestiferously human,
As if to infestate inner skin,

They question, almost with a triumph,
When are you going to Maine?
As if you were going to Heaven
And they would see you there!

And you say, yes we are going,
Harsh to be indefinite,
Yes, we are going, we are going,
Yes, we are going to Maine.

SPITE FENCE

After years of bickerings

Family one
Put up a spite fence
Against family two.

Cheek by cheek
They couldn't stand it.
The Maine village

Looked so peaceful.
We drove through yearly,
We didn't know.

Now if you drive through
You see the split wood,
Thin and shrill.

But who's who?
Who made it,
One side or the other?

Bad neighbors make good fencers.

SURVIVORS

Superior elan
Sometimes offends.
One cannot stand it.
To be clear

In mind and body,
Dominating
A scene at eighty-eight

Makes one think
Too much
On height elan,
Abateless ability,

Breaks reality
Into a special claim
On the nature of man,
Especially of women

Who live longest,
Sometimes an eagle-gilt eye
Surveying the scene
From elan,

Elan's proud claim,
Gives dismay
If humility
Exists,

And if it does not,
Gives dismay
Anyway,
Because

The people suffer,
Have credible
Troubles,
Real heartbreak,

And death comes too soon
To any of them,
These sufferers,
Lauded commoners,

Yet ancient ladies,
Graceful, elegant-pictorial,
Eke on,
Drive from Boston to Maine

At ninety,
Play golf at ninety
At Castine,
A way from sorrow,

It is no ambage
To see these etched beings,
Who have evaded ill
By some mysterious principle

We do not know,
High-spirited,

They spring me
Into empathy

With those who have suffered and lost,
With imperfection,
The common lot,
Nature ruthless,

But the theme of this poem
Is that nature is
Not ruthless to them,
Seemingly,

To have joy at ninety,
Ability to drive a car
Three hundred miles without fatigue
Ought to be celebrated.

I am bemused,
I have seen too much love
Gone wrong,
Lives wasted by time,

Am challenged
By too much
Goddess control,
I cannot accept

That to live long means truth
When I think
Of Keats, of Hopkins,
Of Dylan Thomas.

"I hope to see you next year"
Comes across the bay,
A common report
Carried across the water

On an evening still and full
Of falling sunlight by the ocean.
Of course we do
We all do,

We want five chick swallows
In a nest
Under the areaway
To prosper,

And as the mother and father
Gather bugs
And stuff them
In yellow mouths

We watch the process
Until one day
Five swallows
Take their maiden flight.

They make it
Up to the rooftree,
Sit there expectant,
While mother and father

Fly in to feed them
Still; the next night
They retreat
Near the nest,

Bunched five in a row,
Fed still,
A revelation,
How splendid.

Even after mid-July,
The full moon,

The parents feed the young,
Teaching them to fly.

The laws of nature
Are from ancient time,
Why then
Not salute

Old ladies full of grace
Who have
Outwitted time,
Or so it seems,

Continue sportively
Guessing, truthward, at
Genes, environment,
Will, and chance.

FOG I

Fog may be total or partial or light.
When it is total, without wind or waves,
It is less dangerous than with wind or waves.

Off Dog Island in total fog with ten aboard
Dikkon hit a lobster pot. Experience
Stopped the motor instantly. He threw out the anchor.

The vessel was not likely to drift down on the island.
He put the ladder over the stern, drew breath,
Dived under the vessel with enough eyesight to see,

Assessed the situation, came up for breath,
Four immersions allowed him to free the line
Wrapped around the propeller, and to ascend,

Professionally done in cold water without a knife.
They hoisted the anchor, penetrated impenetrable fog,
Made it to safe mooring on Cape Rosier.

FOG II

The implications of fog are enormous.
If you cannot see, what can you see?
The idea of the blindness of mankind.

The father says to the son, do not go.
It is foolhardy on the ocean to go in the fog.
Mariners in Maine have deep respect for the fog.

The son says to the father, I am young.
You always told me not to go in the fog,
But when I returned you praised my ability.

The son went through the impenetrable fog
Because he was young, in some way foolishly.
The young mariner loved a sense of adventure.

The young wrest control from their elders
And take their lives in their hands on the sea,
The elders wait, hope they will make it to shore.

EAGLES

To Allen Tate

Eagles, symbols of our state, lordly birds
Whose wide wings expertly feather air,
Depleted by chemicals we supplied,
Are intractable to write about.

Who would be an eagle? Imperious mien,
Have you seen them traversing the skies?
Majestic sight! Have you seen their talons,
Powerful to subdue enemies?

Hard to adjust to the idea of an eagle!
We fly eagles above our flag.
We have banished them to Alaska. Our division
Is so deep we dare not look at them.
The high! The American ideal! The eagles!

Their eyes, agile, are lofty, specific.
They see more than we, overseers of
Fierce direct gaze beyond duality.
They live beyond the reach of intellect.

This magnificent bird addresses me
With his spirit liable to death.
As the ocean surveillance of the poetic,
If an eagle spirit dies, poetry dies.
If an eagle spirit lives, man flies.

MAINE SUMMER
HIGH COLOR LUNCHEON

Sufficiently high over Muscongus Bay
Looking afar to islands, open ocean subverted,
Blues, whites, greens dazzling the eyesight, and
Flowers telling their truth, elders
Gather on the lawn in high, dry, clean, light air,
Matisse-striped, before a table of drinks
Of reflective colors, radishes, carrots, cauliflowers,
Onions, vegetable efflorations, lobster sandwiches,

Persons survivors of shredded decades,
Philanthropist, governor, teacher, painter,

Looking complex, one cancer-abated,
Coming to the highland island by outboard power
Agilely evading lobster pots, persons bright characters
Streaked in knowledge of separation, marriage, divorce,
Children, grandchildren, flecked by gauzy light,
Hummingbirds thought red sugar-water flasks real flowers.

FOG I

Fog depends on density, but so does man.
Now you can see *Reve* in the bay, with
Attendant boats, now scarcely, now you cannot.

Man depends on the density of his knowledge,
But finally it is blackout. He was bright,
But fog moved in occluding his spirit.

Pleasant to sit on the land looking at the fog
On the sea. Will it lift, or be total occlusion?
Fog moves in and out, ideas move in and out.

Fog brings on a stealthy quietude, through which
A sea bell speaks far out, or, near, a sea gull.
Quiet of earth before the storm of birth.

Total density is total invisibility.
After life, we must be in a total fog.
Forever quiet, but this won't last forever.

After some time, the clamor of high sunlight,
Far bright looks, action, the speeches of men.
In fog you thought you knew something irremediable.

FOG II

Clarity is the excellence of rationality.
Socrates in the agora was not fogged in.
Plato and Aristotle could be explicit in their ways.

We use a word like glory for clarity,
We use a word like chaos for madness,
Some great men have been mad, some sane.

If I sit in the fog, looking at the fog, not
Seeing through the fog, how clear can I be?
By imagination I can be clear as in clear sunlight.

But then, in sunlight I could be metaphorically fogged.
What, then, is the controlling principle? Nature,
Nature is the master of man, nature controls him.

I cannot ask the fog to go away, to vanish,
I cannot ask a sunny day to turn to fog,
I can ask, who am I, what am I doing in the world?

SEA STORM

Evening at the calm,
That's the best of all.
The seas quiet enough to think.
Not to have to combat them.
They are so much stronger than
Man they could kill him.
He survives, and triumphs, for a time,
By chance and wit. Wit to foresee
The fall of the barometer,
The danger of old charts,
Too many aboard,
Lack of ship-to-shore CB,

Lack of a young mariner
In case old ones
Have a heart attack,
The sea
Is not interested
In the pleasures of summer folk.

Evening at the calm,
If it would only stay still
Like this,
The full tide coming in
With a slight breeze,
The tide extraordinarily full
Under a full moon in July,
The moment of stasis
I praise,

I could tell you tales of the sea
And will tell you one.
At four o'clock
On an August afternoon
With a heavy southwester blowing,
Timmy Rhodes appeared,
A calm man on the coast of Maine,
Owner of Beach Island down Penobscot Bay,
And said,
Would you take me out in *Reve,*
My son may be lost in the storm.
He left Beach Island in the morning
In a slight dinghy with an outboard,
Has not been seen since.
He may be washed up on an island
Between Beach and the mainland,
Will you go search for him?

We knew there was not much light left.
We said sure, let's go. Timmy and I, and

Jackson Brodsky, six feet six, and our dog,
Boarded the cruiser *Reve* in heavy weather,
I with misgivings, but hopeful to find Timmy's son,
And took off toward Spectacle Island.
We searched the shore, found no body or boat.
We headed for Fiddle Head and Hog Island,
The seas were high but still island-repulsed.
We searched Hog and Fiddle Head.
When we got beyond Hog heading for Beach Island
The full weight of the storm bore on us,
From the West over the Camden Hills,
To left and right a hundred miles of ocean
Came at us in a red ominous light of sun
And man-chewing fury.
We took the seas on our starboard quarter.
Half across
Tons of water crashed into the after cockpit,
Fortunately self-bailing,
Whereupon Timmy said,
With the calm of an old New Englander,
"I wouldn't let that happen again."
I had heard the phrase about
Shivering the timbers. *Reve's* timbers shivered,
She rose up and shook off the heavy waters
Piling over her and into her,
One stood fast at the wheel, all one could do.
I plied the cruiser like a sailing vessel,
Turning her into the highest waves,
Searching out any point of vantage,
We had faith in our vessel,
But knew to expect any eventuality.
The red sea in all its might and selfhood,
A deadly sight of malevolent oncome,
Total affront, how could we survive this,
Yet we kept on through the forcing waves
At low speed, and came to Beach Island
Where the storm was so strong,

33

The waves so high, we could not
Pick up a mooring, had to
Head her into the wind,
Keep the engine going, keep her
Head on, direct against danger of sidestroke,
And how long could we do this?

Timmy, fearful for his son,
Wanted to get off,
Go by dinghy to Lisa Jane,
Insisted he would not give up
But search the islands for his son.
We didn't think he could get off,
How he got off I'll never know
but he did, and rowed to Lisa Jane,
Took off in lording seas to find his son.
We might never see him again.

Now the light was leaving, we had
Only about an hour, and had to decide
Whether to seek the leeward of Beach
And anchor for the night, in the tearing,
Tear-forcing storm,
Which we knew not whether it would
Get worse or abate,
So we left perilous stasis
Of heading into the wind
And a hundred miles of red, hard-evil seas,
And got around to the lee.
It all seemed desperate.

We finally decided
That since we had crossed from Hog to Beach
And taken tons of water,
But survived,
We had better chance it again,
Get home by nightfall in half an hour

Rather than chance
A slippery anchor
And the unknown terrors of the night.

So we headed *Reve* into the storm,
Now with the wind and the waves on our port,
And tried her through the waves
Evading the big ones turning into them.
It was a poker passage but we made it,
Some lee help from Fiddle and Spectacle,
And brought *Reve* to mooring at Undercliff,
Just before dark.

The father who might have lost his son at sea,
Timmy, appeared later at Undercliff by car
From Buck's Harbor, with his tall son, who,
His motor conked out, took off his shirt and
Made a sail in the dinghy and in the high wind
And seas, a young man sure of himself, fearless,
Sailed into Buck's Harbor miles away,
Hardy and able, evading death, even happy,
And Timmy had scoured the faceless seas,
Not found his son or his boat,
And directed Lisa Jane into Buck's Harbor,
Where was his boy
Luckily out of the predation of the ghastly waters.

We had a round of drinks
To fortune,
That happened to turn out good that day.

CLIFF

Through years of valiant schemes and dreams
He struggled to the top; vice-president now
Of a large advertising company of New York.
His father had been football coach at Town.
He tussled life like a bulldog with a bone.
He married a blond tall woman from the South
And now they had three children growing up.

In ice-blue waters of a Maine July
A line became fouled in the propeller
And rudder of the cruiser; probably wound
Around the propeller shaft before the engine stopped.
Cliff answered the call for help, stripped
To white trunks, went over the side and under
To see what he could do where others failed.

He went down under the vessel twenty times
If he went once. He could not be kept up.
Massed, cold blue water quickly blued his lips
But he would dive down, after a breathing space,
Again, and again. Others were good for once
Or twice, but Cliff would not give up, tantalized
To sullen fascination before the difficult.

We'd pull him up, after prolonged exertion,
Saying, 'Cliff, Cliff, stay up, you'll have a heart attack.'
But he attacked the undersides once more,
Disdaining advice in tenacious drives and dives.
After an hour and a half he freed the line,
He shook a bone-white smile at us, threw high
His hands, and sailed away, and married a Greek woman.

A LOON CALL

Rowing between Pond and Western Islands
As the tide was coming in
Creating, for so long, two barred islands,
At the end of August, fall nip in the air,
I sensed something beyond me,
Everywhere I felt it in my flesh
As I beheld the sea and sky, the day,
The wordless immanence of the eternal,
And as I was rowing backward
To see directly where I was going,
Harmonious in the freedom of the oars,
A solitary loon cry locked the waters.

Barbaric, indivisible, replete with rack,
Somewhere off where seals were on half-tide rocks,
A loon's cry from beyond the human
Shook my sense to wordlessness.

Perfect cry, ununderstandable essence
Of sound from aeons ago, a shriek,
Strange, palpable, ebullient, wavering,
A cry that I cannot understand,
Praise to the cry that I cannot understand.

FAT SPIDER

Thrills, the fat spider
Who comes only in September,
What was she doing in July,

While swallows were nesting
Above a lightbulb in our areaway,
Produced their chicks, who flew away.

37

While people were coming and going,
Sailors sailing,
Poets making poems,

What was the fat spider doing
Who came out only in September,
As she had each year and years ago?

The fat spider, intelligent,
As nature, wordless, impinges,
Knew when to appear,

Appeared outside my study window,
Twenty paces from the ocean,
To astonish me to her acceptance,

She took glory in existence
Constructing her web in iridescence
As a map of the universe

Rain came down over the roof
But she had calculated nicely
To spin between the roof and the window.

There the fat spider, queenly,
Ordered her natural existence,
Big and dangerous, fat and sleek,

And caught me off my thinking base,
Because she was so inevitably clean
She would kill everything within reach.

ALL OF US

Fortified by a piece of paper
The spirit rages in me inconsolable
But what shall I write on the paper?

Shall I say life is magnificent,
All have known moments of magnificence,
Because a moment was magnificent?

Shall I say life is inordinately brief,
Because Mozart lived only thirty-five years
Or that Chatterton lived not two decades?

Shall I say that grief is heavier, more durable
than happiness, and will never be outlived,
And some sufferings cannot be put into words?

Shall I say that Julia Gray, in open casket yesterday,
Who lived to be ninety-one, knew joy and sorrow,
Is not a mystery to existence, like all of us?

Like all of us we are pulled by forces
Greater than we could control, or evaluate,
Time was our enemy who seemed to be our friend,

Fate was our history, to be and not to be,
We were a grain of order in a sea of chance,
Rose and thorn, spirit and matter, life and death.

GOING

The comfortable craggy slope
You go up through knotted roots.
There is a long spell of walking
With little or no talking.

39

It is a long climb you are making,
A severe journey you are taking,
Under a canopy of twisted trees
Through which you can see the summer sea.

The sea is there in the distance,
You are aware of its existence
As you climb to the goal on the hill,
Something you can do if you will.

It has been done many times before,
Constricted road to an open door.
You brought what you had in your heart
Long before the arduous start.

Some came heavily, some came lightly,
Some have insight, some have no sight,
Some have nothing left to tell
After they have heard the warning bell.

A descent down the moss and rock face
Was necessary from that high place
Down into doubts, uncertainties
In a world of depths of mysteries.

DEEP FISHING

Poetry is like fishing,
If you have six hooks
On a line one hundred feet down

What you have to do
Is wait for carp to strike,
A mystery of no feeling.

Haul up every half hour,
Often the bright beings
Are there, colorful catch.

You are way out in the ocean.
Percy is showing you how to fish.
In the distance is Egg Rock.

Whether strike or no strike
The ocean remains the same.
It is careless of you.

The ocean is the sea
Of creativity, dark down deep.
Memory is the line.

A caught fish is a poem
From the depths. Sometimes
They come, sometimes not.

The depths have made them virile
In their way. You are fishing,
Poetry is possible.

Fish die soon,
Poetry may live,
Ocean of imagination.

Percy starts up the motor.
If we go by Eagle Island light
We'll be in by dark.

Our boat was full of poems
That timeless summer day
So long ago.

ON THE 100TH BIRTHDAY
OF SCOTT NEARING

AUGUST 6, 1983

Today is my 100th birthday
I outlasted them all.
But now I die, here now I fall.

I spoke when I had fire
For peace, justice, freedom.
What is there now to desire?

Friends come with banners to my couch,
Not yet quite a bier,
Sing songs by the Penobscot.

I can hardly make them out.
Helen, only eighty, tries to make me
Wake to the songs of the free

I fought for all my life, a child
One month old kisses my cheek
Not knowing what she is doing.

The contradictions are too great.
They place a wreath of flowers
On my head and on Helen's

As I enter my second century.
A year ago I was sawing, stacking wood,
My books were read around the world.

Here I lie unable to comprehend
The love these friends bring toward the end
Of a life devoted to making mankind better.

Against avarice, special privilege I staked my claim
And gave my love and work to the common man,
May the Republic survive, knowing my effort.

And what was a tune they sang?
New words of praise. Guess what,
The Battle Hymn of the Republic.

VIGNETTE
Achievement, Ninth Symphony
For Philip Booth

Standing amid the alien corn
Ruth Adams made a hole in one
At ninety on the golf course at Castine,
Went home, into the black hole herself that night.

SUMMER INCIDENT

Leo, Pekingese with tiny legs and imperial will
Strode across the stony beach for ten years, body

Of love able to cope with anything human,
Taken for granted as a fixed force of nature,

Everyone loved Leo, fierce and small, quaint and strong,
He could hold his own in face of vicissitude,

Reliable and eager, close-known to all the cottagers,
Sometimes barking in triumph at the great ocean.

Leo instructed mankind in the headiness of survival,
With other dogs he seemed to have no rival.

One day Leo's master, just recovering from a heart attack,
Leashed the elegant creature to walk up to the mailbox.

Suddenly Jack's big black dog, supposed to be house-held,
Who had once showed hatred of tiny Leo,

Rushed out of the house with incredible speed,
With furious eye and grimness straight to Leo.

His master instantly pulled tiny Leo up to his chest,
The great black dog leaped up, fiercely bit and tore,

Not knocking the man down, blood all over the place,
The master forced the dog off, friends bore bleeding Leo

In a station waggon to the nearest vet, miles away,
But he died enroute, they turned and brought him back.

The neighbors, summer people, were soon enraged,
Called for a death for a death. Jack took a shotgun

Down the cove to Percy's shack, the big dog chained,
Told old Percy to put a bullet through his head.

Soon from half a mile away a small crowd standing around
Heard two shots ring out on the clear afternoon air,

Percy, the old keeper, shovelled him in behind his shack.
Next day there was a service high up on the mountain.

Leo was partially covered by a blanket, his eyes open.
He was wide-eyed and as peaceful as if sleeping.

A dozen men and women picked at the stony ground
To make a half-foot deep grave for an intrepid friend.

They laid him in, blanket and all, placed a crude wooden marker,
Silence, not a dry eye among the group of homo sapiens.

They were witness to starkness, the cruelty of nature,
Aware of their own deaths, come as they may.

He was killed on the breast of man,
Man thinks he lives on the breast of God.

DOG DAYS

A group of homo sapiens all weeping
Stand around the grave of a dog
Half way up the mountain. The earth
Was so hard it took shovels and picks
Half an hour to dig a shallow hole.

We put a heavy stone on top of the grave
To keep one dog from eating another.

A year later there was no sign of the grave.
If you walk up the ferny path you wouldn't know.

If you walk to the top you can pick blueberries,
Look beyond green islands to open blue ocean.

CHART INDENT

Ile Au Haut is way down there in the distance,
Given a particular kind of day, and if
You are not afraid of the ocean, have daring,
A stout boat and a stout heart

You might sail from here due South,
Pass Eagle Island Light, go into open
Ocean and make for Stonington, if plucky
Continue south to the high island.

Long before getting to Roaring Bull Ledge
Facing the open Atlantic, this
Open enough, you might find a small opening in
The chart and map of the watery world

And there find safe harbor, secure your vessel,
Cast anchor in a safe place, be warned by a native
Not to come far in, the out tide will strand you,
The sea is even treacherous in here, be careful.

You count on the treachery of the sea as endless,
You will haunt her, but you know that every year
She claims lives indifferently, you to be sagacious
And always try to outwit her. Duck in to Duck Harbor,

Sleep snug in sleek harbor, and when dawn comes
Awake to be going out into the ocean
As ancestors have done since time began
And hope you will make safe landfall.

LOOKING OUT

Ah, yes, the same old question
The lack of a sufficient vocabulary.
There must be something beyond the natural landscape.
Seascapes even. Way off Eagle Island Light. Way off
North Haven. As far as the eye can see. Twenty sea miles
Clear as the sea bells. What words for anything more?

Thousands of years ago some sailors, who knows why
Or how, left marks on stone on Crow Island, offshore

From our mainland, words or images marked on stone,
Our best brains think it may mean safe harbor.
This is a sound thing that I was thinking of
But in more spiritual terms. Here it is real.

In spiritual terms how can you figure out the world?
What are our queries about the universe?
Interesting idea, what was the cave man really like?
They must have been more intelligent than we are
Because they did not invent the atom bomb. They wanted
To live, ancestors to our suicidal potential.

Our scientists figure how to blow us apart.
I am not dead yet but have survived five wars.
What is man? How noble in reason, that is to laugh.
We sacrificed the idea of nobility long ago
To greed and gain. Poetry cannot change the view.
Look out! It is the same view the pre-Vikings saw.

DEATH OF A FRIEND

I

Something has changed completely,
    You wouldn't believe it.

The light in the eye, the lift of form,
Hale greetings, the quick steps of dance.

You wouldn't believe it,
    Change has come completely.

Expected references, social situations.
Friendship, movement of life's interplay.

We are up against something beyond us,
    Irreversable change.

II

The word will break too, as unreasonable,
And vanish thin into air,

The poem will be broken and disappear
Forever and a day.

The lovely music of her being
Will be silent as a night.

We are forced to comprehend,
   Abandoned to insight.

MAINE AUGUST SEASIDE EVENING

A granite wound.
Would that be harsh enough?
What is a granite wound?

It is something made by earth
Much harder than the human flesh.
Actually, flesh is soft.

If the world is that hard
Why is flesh that soft?
Shakespeare tried to answer.

The result is tragedy.
But then there is comedy.
Which is hard, which soft?

Mr. Goldhead Superchild is
Already putting elders to shame.
Freud said at three we knew everything.

His sister, equally overt,
Seizes the second page of this poem,
Makes a paper arrow which flies.

Does the poem fly, or the paper?
Something is always going underground.
The underground used to be radical essence.

The underground would teach us how to live.
Is flight to or from? What will these kids
Make of the twenty-first century?

MOMENT THAT STAYS,
BUT PASSES

Eagle Island light stands down the bay
Twelve miles away, imperturbable, innately secret,
Opening out into the drama of muscled ocean,
Hundreds of years are nothing to these waters.

Boats circle slowly, catching mackerel, the
Mackerel are running, the human hunters follow
Without emotion, pulling in the knife-like bright ones.
Old ritual, good for breakfast in the morning.

The sun stands to descend slowly into the treetops,
The silence is compelling, the light on cliffs magnetic,
The serenity of jewelled calm at high tide in the evening
Assumes an attitude of impersonality, innate perfection.

If gulls call far off faintly, an osprey far above
Circles in his necessity, cormorants fly low to Spectacle,
If the majesty and mystery of the universe
Are thoughts in the mind, and if you cannot

Undo the extravagant slow time before sundown,
Reaching back to passion, turmoil, suffering and death,
You have to breathe this as a moment of perfection
Like the touch of a lover in an afternoon in a park.

Now the slow gradations of time pertain
As the sun descends and as the night approaches,
Man's cultivation of the world, of green enclosures,
Gives way and hold to dangerous darkness

Where if we sleep we are like the dead,
And when we wake we suffer struggle and fate,
But for a moment, twilight between life and death,
We live in a love that is now, and embrace it.

A strange, miraculous color of deepening shade
Alerts the eye to the relativity of time,
A thousand years ago the scene was the same,
Love of the world permanent and impermanent.

GULLED

It is said that man is gulled but I
Experienced the bit experience anew today
When a gull at lowest tide gulled me.

He also gulled Rick and Dr. Brown.
He seemed a young gull of this summer, dark
Not yet lighter, with one feather sticking out

Of one wing, which seemed excuse for not flying.
Rick and Dr. Brown were in kayaks, I afoot.
The gull would not take off. He paddled ashore.

Rick and Dr. Brown were paddling by the shore.
I walked down the shingle, daring to catch a bird in hand.
The bird walked off the seaweed, paddled by the bald rock

High out of water at low tide, which it now was.
I signalled to Rick and Dr. Brown to box him in
Against the high side of the steep egg rock.

We were three human beings, two in kayaks,
One walking, predators of a broken gull.
Something had been broken in the gull or he would go.

I really did not know what I wanted to do.
Did I want to catch this large wild bird in my hands?
Had we three any reason to interfere with nature?

It is important to assert that no malice
Existed in the hearts of three members of mankind
Curious about the inability of a gull to fly.

Curiosity, yes. Yes, a wish, somehow, how, to help.
None of the three knew the outcome of the drama.
If the wing broken, death the sooner the better, we thought

We thought. Nature exists in wordless impersonality.
Our little boxing-in operation began to fail
As the young gull began paddling out to sea

While the kayakers adjusted their oars and the landsman
Was still going out up to his knees. Then the sea gull,
With an abrupt indifference, an absolute disdain

Of man's concern for his welfare, raised his wings to the air,
Not maimed, not broken, not death-warranted,
Sailed out lowly over the bay in measured grace

And rose to the height of the other gulls of his society,
Flew with conclusions not to be foregone,
While all three of us felt gulled, each with different reasons.

THE IMMORTAL PICTURE

I want that picture, the perfect view
Of vessels outside our house riding easy,
Great ocean eventuated by islands,
A spectacle of order, harmony, and control

When we know everything is changeful and mortal,
We know the immortal picture is false,
The perfect view will not last,
Change comes on, good turns to bad,
Evil lurks in every picture of man,
Even though we have a good view for Christmas.

The beautiful body decays, the
Beautiful mind is destroyed, the
Great and powerful go to death,

The times change, the poem ends,
The poem ends because heartbreak
Overcomes human beings
Because they cannot control the world.
After twelfth night
We threw the Christmas tree over the cliff.

LIGHT AND DARK

Such a beautiful day.
I like the light.
So much destruction everywhere.

The light is
New England changeable,
Changes fast.

The blacks are fighting blacks,
The Jews are fighting Jews,
the whites have always been fighting whites.

The light is
Better than darkness
Yet remarkably the same.

Such a beautiful day.
I like the light.
I wish it would go on forever.

The hundred year olds
Are playing bridge,
Fighting across the table.

The poets are always
Writing, writing, writing,
Inditing, inditing, inciting.

So much destruction everywhere.
Why do men fight?
They kill each other all the time.

Such a beautiful day.
I like the light,
Dark of the dawn.

SUN-MAKE

The sun, arising to a flawless day
Shines on the right side of the vessels
Since the slight wind is from the north

And finds a strange single puff of clouds,
Bright white, at the far horizon to the south,
The only clouds in the perfect early day,

Making an astonishing effect not seen before
For there across the water and on it
In perfect silence, stillness, long pause,

Is a gigantic mirror of clouds down on
The ocean, as if impossible to be there,
Immaculately great, statuesque and static.

In all the years he had seen this vast scene
This new phenomenon was astonishing, unique,
A mysterious new shape in the universe.

This puff of clouds, mirrored so far away
In a way that could not be imagined
Made for thought beside the morning blue ocean,

It was a system of light and distance so exquisite
He thought it should remain perfectly wordless,
Then the sky changed, he changed his mind, shaped this.

WAITING TO LEAN
TO THE MASTER'S COMMAND

Three boats headed Northeast, moored,
Look like greyhounds straining at the leash.
They wish to go, but have no will of their own
Whether night or day, tide in or tide out.

These exquisite creatures have no imagination,
They cannot go to sea, to any harbor,
They have to wait on the command of man,
Man says go, they go, moving on Penobscot Bay.

SAILING TO BUCK'S HARBOR

The spectacle of the New York Yacht Club
Coming into Buck's Harbor
After diminution of the wind,
Lateral sun rays held on expressive hulls,

Ingathers yacht lovers in late summertime.

Old-timers linger on the lawn
Cocktail-handling, remembering

A same sight similarly suitable
Of tall ships coming in long ago

Before north sundown, now grandchildren are here,
Before the yacht club lecture,

"Sailing to Tahiti."

GOING BACKWARD GOING FORWARD

For Andrews Wanning

Toccata's sails were up and set,
We were coming in from undefined ocean

To the beginning of large and small islands
Worked through before coming to far landfall.

Toccata, elegant and able at sea-play,
Lived on the waters with living joy, when

I noticed a marker to starboard going forward.
Impossible, we were going backward going forward.

Electrified at this astonishing revelation of the sea
We sat there peering expectantly toward the mainland

While we were slowly being carried backward out to sea,
Seeming wind outdone by currents and the tide

That kept Toccata shaped elegantly to the North
While, gently daft, Toccata slipped directly aft.

We were being sent beyond our wills backward South,
Slowly backward, engraved on ocean, far out.

STONE FENCE

They are sitting on a stone fence by a mall.
They have the youth and good looks of the mid-twenties.
Beside them rises a new building of brick and steel.
The jack hammers have just ceased making a big noise.

They seem innocent, adequate, and are certainly childless.
They do not look at each other with fervor or supplication.
They look as if they took life for granted, were sure
Of the langorous hills surrounding the old town.

A zealot who is totally alive to reality,
Aware of an election coming up almost at once,
Seeing these extravanantly detached lollers,
Asks them why they do not go next door and vote.

A citizen should vote for one side or another,
Take sides, be active, know what the world is doing.
They looked blissful sitting on a stone fence,
These young people went on munching candy bars.

These two were as it were out of history.
They did not seem to take part in the system.

You knew they would get up and drive or walk home
Without the slightest knowledge of the fall of Rome.

CLOUDS

Clouds so big you would think they are the rosy bosoms
Of young girls. How could the old world look so new?
They stand up as if they had their own being,
But are only pushed by the wind, and break into new forms.

The new forms are equally expressive, and before long
The girls grow up and have children, grow to be old ladies
While every day the skies present some new wonder
Of unique cloud shapes making the heart to leap and bound.

Bound over the billows? Bound into the pillows?
We are bound to lose as time takes us away
Leaving a few poems to make their way in the world
To establish fundamental wonder and astonishment.

For it is all so old, and all so new, life,
The obsessive careful prosody, ancient structures
Of linguistic images to control life for love,
If you don't control it love will run away with you.

LOOKING AT THE WATERS

Can you say anything new about looking at the waters?
The wind and the water, the tides, very old, very new.
The tide is coming to the full at eventide, full tide,
The wind is lessening, the waves are lessening, now

A grand quiet comes over the universe,
The sun yet up, the full moon yet to come,

Reve and Maddy B. are riding on their moorings,
Five other boats are subject to strange currents.

Maddy B. and Reve are pointing west at sundown,
Within five minutes they are pointing east, others
Are in between. It is the currents make them go,
Oddly sometimes in opposite directions.

I wish I could figure out the nature of the world,
Why one boat heads one way, why one heads another,
What is the current that shapes our direction,
Our disposition, law seems to rule the vessels.

What law binds us and what law frees us
And what can we know about ultimate forces
As we sit between birth and death looking at water
Moved as it is and we are by inscrutable forces?

We do not have answers to ultimate questions
As we sit by the shore at eventide seeing the sea,
Just as we accept mankind, its history,
Just as we do not know its ultimate possibility,

No moment is so good as a sure moment
When words take on a supernatural mystery,
And wherever the sea and we are going,
Ultimately the best is in not knowing,